ANGEL ISLAND

Tom Greve

Rourke
Educational Media

rourkeeducationalmedia.com

Scan for Related Titles
and Teacher Resources

D0565139

Before Reading:

Building Academic Vocabulary and Background Knowledge

Before reading a book, it is important to tap into what your child or students already know about the topic. This will help them develop their vocabulary, increase their reading comprehension, and make connections across the curriculum.

1. *Look at the cover of the book. What will this book be about?*
2. *What do you already know about the topic?*
3. *Let's study the Table of Contents. What will you learn about in the book's chapters?*
4. *What would you like to learn about this topic? Do you think you might learn about it from this book? Why or why not?*
5. *Use a reading journal to write about your knowledge of this topic. Record what you already know about the topic and what you hope to learn about the topic.*
6. *Read the book.*
7. *In your reading journal, record what you learned about the topic and your response to the book.*
8. *After reading the book complete the activities below.*

Content Area Vocabulary
Read the list. What do these words mean?

allies
barracks
complicated
hardships
humiliation
immigrants
immigrating
Industrial Revolution
legacy
lure
preservationists
recession

After Reading:

Comprehension and Extension Activity

After reading the book, work on the following questions with your child or students in order to check their level of reading comprehension and content mastery.

1. *What were some other uses for Angel Island? (Summarize)*
2. *What are some reasons people would leave one country for another? (Asking Questions)*
3. *Why would Chinese immigrants go through Angel Island in California instead of Ellis Island in New York? (Inferring)*
4. *Why do you think the Chinese had a hard time entering the United States? (Asking Questions)*
5. *Were the Chinese the only immigrants to pass through Angel Island? Explain. (Summarize)*

Extension Activity

What is your family history? The United States is a nation made up of immigrants. Nearly every family in the U.S. has started someplace else, usually another country. Interview your family members. Where did your grandparents come from? Your great- grandparents? Why did people in your family move from place to place? Create a map that shows your family history as they moved from country to country, state to state, or town to town.

TABLE OF CONTENTS

Chapter 1

PEOPLE AND PLACES

When Americans sing the National Anthem, we hail our country as the land of the free and the home of the brave.

Brave people from all over the world have been coming to the United States seeking freedom and opportunity throughout the nation's history. Some places in the U.S. have become symbols of that bravery.

The First Americans

Nearly every historic site in the United States sits on land first inhabited by Native Americans. While U.S. History reaches back hundreds of years, Native Americans were living there long before that.

Like giant beacons, New York's Statue of Liberty and the massive presidential carvings at South Dakota's Mount Rushmore celebrate the United States while also preserving its history. They are two of the most recognized symbols of freedom.

California's Angel Island is a place where many people came from other countries, seeking freedom and opportunity. It sits near the mouth of California's San Francisco Bay.

Angel Island

Despite covering just 1.2 square miles (3.1 square kilometers), Angel Islands location near the Pacific Ocean has made it a valuable piece of land since before California even became a state in 1850.

Its role in the country's history is unique. Angel Island is where the hopes and dreams of thousands of people who came to America to find a better life were put on hold.

Chapter 2

WHERE ARE YOU FROM?

The history of nearly every person's family in the United States started in another place, or country. This makes the U.S. a nation of **immigrants**.

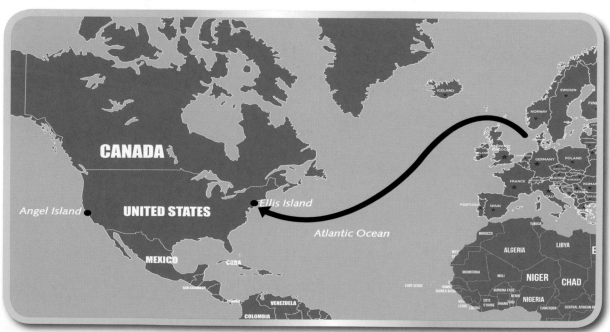

Since the United States began as part of Great Britain, the nation's early history, and its first large waves of immigrants, came across the Atlantic Ocean on ships from Western Europe.

Immigration is hard. It is hard for a person to stop living in one country, move a long distance, and start living in a new country. Despite these **hardships**, people have been **immigrating** to the U.S. throughout its history, and they are still doing it today.

America's Front Door

Starting in the late 1800s, millions of U.S. immigrants arrived at Ellis Island, near New York City, to gain entry into the country. The Island, which is next to the Statue of Liberty, served as a welcome sign for immigrants trying to start a new life in the United States.

Chapter 3

PURSUING AN AMERICAN DREAM

There is almost no limit to the reasons why people immigrate to another country. In the late 1800s and early 1900s, millions of European immigrants poured into the U.S. seeking a better life than what they had in their old country.

Freedom Fact!

*The first massive wave of immigrants coming to America came at least partly to find jobs. New factories in the U.S. needed workers, and many immigrants took a chance that they could find better jobs in the United States. Historians call this period the **Industrial Revolution**.*

Factories like the McFadden Coffee & Spice Company, located in Iowa, hired many immigrants.

Also during this same time, many immigrants from East Asia, on the other side of the world, began coming to the U.S. across the Pacific Ocean.

The same hope of opportunity bringing Europeans to the United States soon brought immigrants from the other side of the world in China. Chinese immigrants crossed the Pacific Ocean rather than the Atlantic and arrived in California.

Angel Island and the Civil War

Camp Reynolds

Despite the fact that most of the fighting in the American Civil War (1861-1865) took place in the eastern half of the country, thousands of miles from California, Angel Island became a Union military base during the War. Camp Reynolds, built on the Island in 1863, became a key part of the Union's defense against Confederate ships trying to enter San Francisco Bay.

Angel Island got its name from Spanish Explorer Juan de Ayala. In 1775 he became the first European to set foot on the Island and called it "The Island of the Angels." The beach where he came ashore remains Ayala Cove to this very day.

By 1905, with immigrants still pouring through Ellis Island back east, the U.S. government opened a second immigration station to process the thousands of Chinese immigrants arriving on the West Coast in California.

Its location and history as a military fort made Angel Island an easy choice to serve as the West Coast's version of Ellis Island. But many of the Chinese immigrants arriving at Angel Island got a much different reception than the immigrants who arrived at Ellis Island.

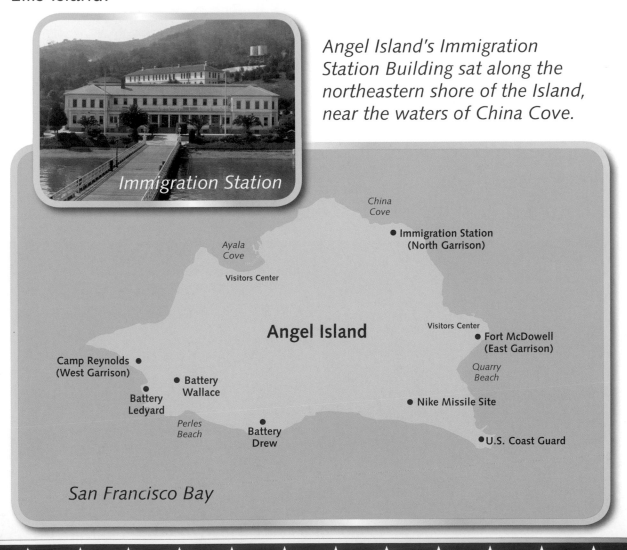

Immigration Station

Angel Island's Immigration Station Building sat along the northeastern shore of the Island, near the waters of China Cove.

China Cove

Ayala Cove

Immigration Station (North Garrison)

Visitors Center

Angel Island

Visitors Center

Fort McDowell (East Garrison)

Quarry Beach

Camp Reynolds (West Garrison)

Battery Wallace

Battery Ledyard

Perles Beach

Battery Drew

Nike Missile Site

U.S. Coast Guard

San Francisco Bay

Chapter 4

AFTER THE GOLD RUSH

The **complicated** history of Chinese immigrants and their experiences at Angel Island has its roots in the California Gold Rush of the late 1840s. Word spread around the world quickly after the 1848 discovery of gold near Coloma, California. Hundreds of thousands of people came not just from the U.S., but from around the world, seeking fortune as gold prospectors.

Gold!

The biggest number of California gold-seekers arrived in 1849. To this day, San Francisco's football team name, the *49ers*, refers to the Gold Rush. So does California's official nickname, *The Golden State*. Even the Golden Gate Bridge, a symbol of freedom in its own right, is a reference to the California Gold Rush.

A **recession** in the 1870s suddenly made jobs hard to find in the U.S. and especially in California where so many people had settled after the Gold Rush. Many Chinese immigrants started working as track-layers for the railroads which were expanding into California.

Many people thought Chinese immigrants were taking the few jobs that did exist because they believed the Chinese would work for very little pay.

The U.S. Immigration Station at Angel Island took in its first Chinese immigrants in 1910. But, for these and many Chinese immigrants who followed, Angel Island became not so much a welcoming station, but more of a trap which could be difficult to leave.

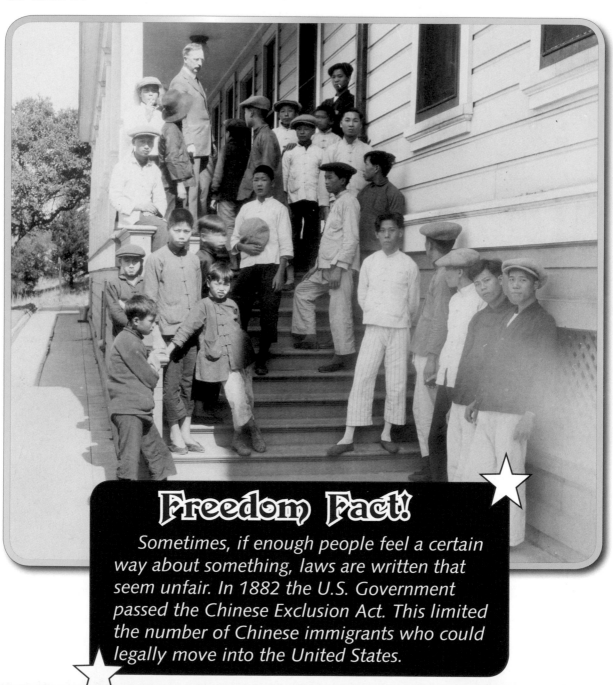

Freedom Fact!

Sometimes, if enough people feel a certain way about something, laws are written that seem unfair. In 1882 the U.S. Government passed the Chinese Exclusion Act. This limited the number of Chinese immigrants who could legally move into the United States.

For the next 30 years, more than 150 thousand immigrants, most of them Chinese, arrived at Angel Island. When European immigrants came to Ellis Island, they were able to leave in a single afternoon. But when Chinese immigrants came to Angel Island they had to stay for weeks, months, and in some cases years, before they could leave the Island and get on with their lives in America.

Other immigrants, including Japanese and Russians, also came to the U.S. through Angel Island. They were not as restricted as the Chinese in their entry to the country.

Chapter 5

IF THESE WALLS COULD TALK

Angel Island's Immigration Station operated until 1940 when a fire destroyed the main office. The **barracks**, where the immigrants lived at the Island, did not burn.

Most Chinese immigrants who passed through Angel Island eventually gained freedom into America. For some, the Angel Island experience was just an inconvenience. For others, it was a life-changing **humiliation**.

In order to leave Angel Island, Chinese immigrants had to answer many questions about who they knew in the U.S., where they were going to live, and what they were going to do. If they could not answer certain questions, they'd be held for more questioning at a later date.

Angel Island

Despite its beauty, Angel Island was isolated. Immigrants held there could not leave the island to visit the city of San Francisco, which they could often see just across the bay.

The Chinese immigrants who were held for weeks, months, or even years at Angel Island documented their experience the only way they could. They began carving verses of poetry on the walls of their barracks.

Over the years, Immigration Station workers covered the Chinese carvings with paint or putty. However, more would appear as more immigrants arrived, still looking for better lives in America.

These poems written at Angel Island speak of the heartbreaking disappointment of many Chinese immigrants. After traveling so far from home, the realization of being denied the freedom and opportunity they sought in America was difficult to bear.

The Voices of Angel Island

Imprisoned in the wooden building day after day,
My freedom is withheld; how can I bear to talk about it?
I look to see who is happy but they only sit quietly.
I am anxious and depressed and cannot fall asleep.
– Author unknown

The waves are happy, laughing "Ha-ha!"
When I arrived on the island, I heard I was
forbidden to land.
I could do nothing but frown and feel angry at heaven.
– Author unknown

I am distressed that we Chinese are
in this wooden building.
I should regret my taking the risks of
coming in the first place.
– Author unknown

The living conditions in the dormitories at Angel Island were cramped and uncomfortable for the Chinese immigrants.

木屋拘留幾十天，
所因國例致牽連。
可惜英雄無用武，
只聽音來身挫轅。

從今遠別此樓中，
各位鄉君眾歡同。
莫道其間容西式，
設成奎動變如籠。

Much of the writing, translated here into English, details both the hopes and hardships of immigration, regardless of where a person comes from. It also details the disappointment that Chinese immigrants experienced during their stay at Angel Island.

Chapter 6

ANGEL ISLAND STATE PARK

By 1943 the U.S. and China became **allies** in World War II and the government repealed the Chinese Exclusion Act. Angel Island was once again property of the U.S. Army.

By the mid-1950s, with World War II over, part of the Island became a State Park. The original size of the state park was 37 acres (15 hectares). The army left the Island for good in 1962 when the Nike missile base was deactivated.

Freedom Fact!

The U.S. military held German and Japanese prisoners of war at Angel Island. One of the prisoners was the captain of one of the small Japanese submarines that attacked the U.S. base at Pearl Harbor. That attack caused the U.S. to enter the war.

Nike Missile Base, Angel Island

Just south of Angel Island sits Alcatraz Island. Alcatraz was a notorious prison believed to be escape-proof. Even if a prisoner could get beyond the prison walls, they still had a mile and a half (2.41 kilometers) of treacherous water to cross in order to gain freedom. Alcatraz prison closed in 1963.

In 1970 the state sent park rangers to inspect the Island's old buildings, expecting to have to tear them down due to decay.

Thirty years after the last Chinese immigrants left Angel Island, park ranger Alex Weiss found the long-forgotten and painted-over carvings they left behind. Through his efforts and the work of state **preservationists**, the carvings and the buildings are still there today.

Today, Angel Island is a beautiful state park with hiking and bike trails, along with an Immigration Museum detailing the Island's role in thousands of immigrants' difficult pursuit of a better life in America. Visitors can still read the immigrants' poems on the walls.

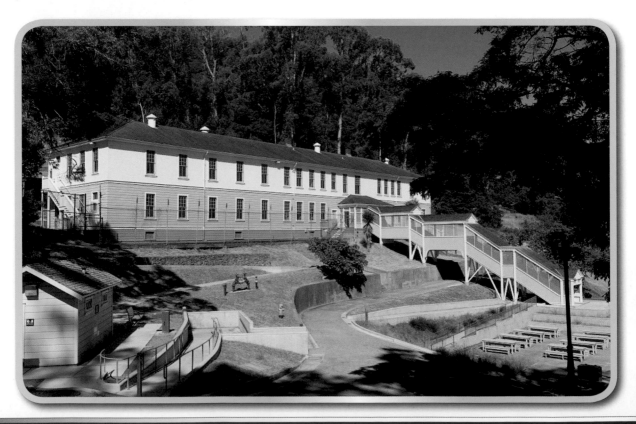

Angel Island has played many roles over its long history. Today its main role is providing a fun place to visit for residents, as well as people visiting the San Francisco Bay Area.

The **lure** of a better life in the United States continues to draw people across its borders. Sometimes, factors beyond any single person's control makes the difficult act of immigration even more complicated. This is the **legacy** of Angel Island, a beautiful but complicated symbol of freedom.

Today, all of Angel Island State Park is open to the public except for a small Coast Guard station on the Island's southeast corner.

TIMELINE

Predating U.S. History into the 1700s – California's Miwok Indians use hand-made canoes to reach the Island. They use it as hunting and fishing grounds.

1775 —— *Spanish Ship* San Carlos, *captained by Juan de Ayala, lands at the Island. The captain calls it "The Island of the Angels." The name sticks.*

1848 and

1849 —— *The Gold Rush causes California's population to rise sharply.*

1863 —— *Camp Reynolds Union Military Fort begins operation to guard San Francisco Bay against Confederate (southern) Navy ships.*

1860s —— *After the Civil War, Camp Reynolds continues as a military fort, housing and training soldiers for fighting Native Americans in the western U.S.*

1882 —— *Chinese Exclusion Act becomes federal law.*

1905 —— *U.S. Government selects Angel Island as its West Coast Immigration Station to process incoming Asian (mostly Chinese) immigrants.*

1910-1940 —— *Angel Island operates as Immigration Station and Chinese immigrant detention facility.*

1941 —— *Island returned to U.S. Army for use as World War II military prison.*

1950s through

1962 —— *Island houses missile launch site as part of the Cold War National defense effort.*

1962 —— *Island's missile site deactivated and California State Parks Service takes over the Island.*

1970 —— *Long-shuttered barracks inspected before demolition, ranger finds historic wall carvings; effort begins to save carvings and entire barracks as part of current-day Immigration Museum.*

2008 —— *Fire burns nearly half the Island but misses Immigration Museum.*

GLOSSARY

allies (AL-eyes): partners on the same side of a conflict

barracks (BAIR-eks): living quarters for large groups of people with little privacy

complicated (COMP-luh-KAY-tehd): the opposite of simple; multi-leveled, not easily solved

hardships (HARD-ships): difficulties, struggles

humiliation (hyoo-MILL-ee-ay-shuhn): a feeling of being unwanted or without merit

immigrants (IM-uh-gruhnts): people who were born in one country, but move to another to live

immigrating (IM-uh-gray-ting): the act of moving from the country of one's birth to another country

Industrial Revolution (in-DUHSS-tree-uhl rev-uh-LOO-shuhn): a period of mass-automation and manufacturing

legacy (LEG-uh-see): lasting impression of a person, place or thing

lure (LOOR): enticement, that which draws people closer to something

preservationists (prez-uhr-VAY-shun-ists): people interested in keeping things which are rare, or historic for future generations to know and enjoy

recession (ri-SEH-shuhn): a period of poor, or zero, economic growth

INDEX

SHOW WHAT YOU KNOW

1. In what year did the Chinese Exclusion Act become a law?

2. Why were Chinese immigrants held so long at Angel Island?

3. How did immigrants document their time at Angel Island?

4. Why did so many immigrants want to come to the United States?

5. How was Ellis Island different from Angel Island?

WEBSITES TO VISIT

www.aiisf.org
www.parks.ca.gov
www.poeticwaves.net

ABOUT THE AUTHOR

Tom Greve lives in Chicago. He is married, has two children, and enjoys reading and writing about U.S. history and geography. San Francisco, the city nearest Angel Island, is among his favorite places to visit in the United States.

Meet The Author!
www.meetREMauthors.com

www.rourkeeducationalmedia.com

PHOTO CREDITS: Cover © Leonard Zhukovsky; Title Page © Lordel; p4, p10, p15, p20, p21, p22, p23, p26 Library of Congress; p5 © gregobagel, © Mary Stephens; p6-7 © Klaas Lingbeek-van Kranen; p 8, p11 © Zarko Cvijovic; p9 © iofoto; p12 © MDRiley, National Park Service, p13, p16, p17, p18 U.S. National Archives and Records Administration; p14 © Eric Broder Van Dyke; p19 © TONO BALAGUER; p24 National Park Service; p25 © franckreporter; p27 © cdrin; p28 © Jenny Solomon

Edited by: Luana Mitten

Cover design by: Renee Brady
Interior design by: Renee Brady

Library of Congress PCN Data

Angel Island / Tom Greve
(Symbols of Freedom)
ISBN 978-1-63430-044-5 (hard cover)
ISBN 978-1-63430-074-2 (soft cover)
ISBN 978-1-63430-103-9 (e-Book)
Library of Congress Control Number: 2014953360

Printed in the United States of America, North Mankato, Minnesota

Also Available as:
ROURKE'S e-Books